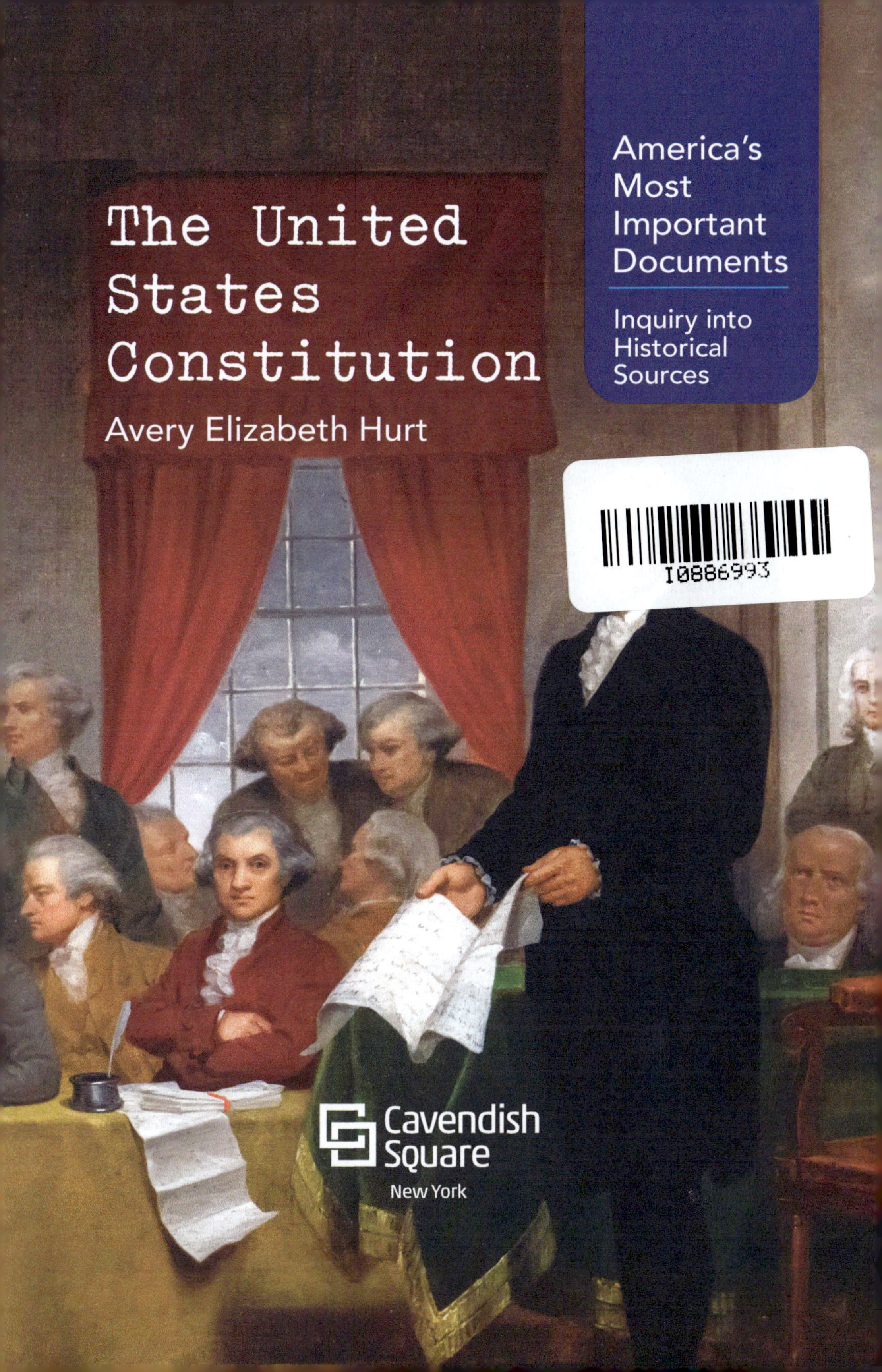

The United States Constitution

Avery Elizabeth Hurt

America's Most Important Documents

Inquiry into Historical Sources

Cavendish Square
New York

Published in 2019 by Cavendish Square Publishing, LLC
243 5th Avenue, Suite 136, New York, NY 10016

First Edition

Library of Congress Cataloging-in-Publication Data

Names: Hurt, Avery Elizabeth, author.
Title: The United States Constitution / Avery Elizabeth Hurt.
Description: First edition. | New York : Cavendish Square, 2018. |
Series: America's Most Important Documents: Inquiry into Historical Sources | Includes bibliographical references and index.
Identifiers: LCCN 2018001786 (print) | LCCN 2018002355 (ebook) | ISBN 9781502636119 (ebook) | ISBN 9781502636102 (library bound) | ISBN 9781502636126 (pbk.)
Subjects: LCSH: United States. Constitution--Juvenile literature. | Constitutional law --United States--Juvenile literature. | United States--Politics and government--1775-1783--Juvenile literature. | United States--Politics and government--1783-1789--Juvenile literature. | Constitutional history--United States--Juvenile literature.
Classification: LCC KF4550 (ebook) | LCC KF4550 .H865 2018 (print) | DDC 342.7302/9--dc23
LC record available at https://lccn.loc.gov/2018001786

Editorial Director: David McNamara
Editor: Kristen Susienka
Copy Editor: Alex Tessman
Associate Art Director: Amy Greenan
Designer: Joe Parenteau
Production Coordinator: Karol Szymczuk
Photo Research: J8 Media

The photographs in this book are used by permission and through the courtesy of: Cover Ian Dagnall/Alamy Stock Photo; p. 4 Haupt Aaron/Science Source/Getty Images; p. 6, 8, 29 North Wind Picture Archives; p. 10 SuperStock Superstock/Getty Images; p. 12 f11photo/Shutterstock.com; p. 13, 20, 24 Bettmann/Getty Images; p. 14 Classic Image/Alamy Stock Photo; p. 17 Steve Heap/Shutterstock.com; p. 18 Joseph Sohm/Corbis/Getty Images; p. 22 David Stuckel/Alamy Stock Photo; p. 25 R. A. Nonenmacher/Wikimedia Commons/File:Iroquois 5 Nation Map c1650.png/Public Domain; p. 31 Derek Bayes/Lebrecht Music and Arts Photo Library/Alamy Stock Photo; p. 32 Samuel Corum/Anadolu Agency/Getty Images; p. 33 Reuters/Newscom; p. 35 Tomwsulcer/Wikimedia Commons/File:Foreign policy US government structure.png/CC0 1.0 Universal Public Domain; p. 38 Jack R Perry Photography/Shutterstock.com; p. 42 Matt McClain/The Washington Post/Getty Images; p. 45 Mireya Acierto/WireImage/Getty Images; p. 46 Library of Congress/Corbis/VCG/Getty Images; p. 49 National Archives/Wikimedia Commons/File:27th Amendment Pg3of3 AC.jpg/Public Domain; p. 50 Harry Hamburg/NY Daily News Archive/Getty Images; p. 52 Tinnaporn Sathapornnanont/Shutterstock.com.

Printed in the United States of America

Contents

We the People of the United States, in Order to form a more perfect

insure domestic Tranquility, provide for the common defence, promote the general Welfare, and secure the Blessing
and our Posterity, do ordain and establish this Constitution for the United States of America.

Article. I.

Section. 1. All legislative Powers herein granted shall be vested in a Congress of the United States, which shall cons
of Representatives.

Section. 2. The House of Representatives shall be composed of Members chosen every second Year by the People of the
in each State shall have the Qualifications requisite for Electors of the most numerous Branch of the State Legislature.

No Person shall be a Representative who shall not have attained to the Age of twenty five Years, and been seven Yea
and who shall not, when elected, be an Inhabitant of that State in which he shall be chosen.

Representatives and direct Taxes shall be apportioned among the several States which may be included within this Unio
Numbers, which shall be determined by adding to the whole Number of free Persons, including those bound to Service for a Term
not taxed, three fifths of all other Persons. The actual Enumeration shall be made within three Years after the first Meeting
and within every subsequent Term of ten Years, in such Manner as they shall by Law direct. The Number of Representat
thirty Thousand, but each State shall have at Least one Representative; and until such enumeration shall be made, the Sta
entitled to chuse three, Massachusetts eight, Rhode Island and Providence Plantations one, Connecticut five, New York s
eight, Delaware one, Maryland six, Virginia ten, North Carolina five, South Carolina five, and Georgia three.

When vacancies happen in the Representation from any State, the Executive Authority thereof shall issue Writs of E

The House of Representatives shall chuse their Speaker and other Officers; and shall have the sole Power of Impea

Section. 3. The Senate of the United States shall be composed of two Senators from each State, chosen by the Legislatur
Senator shall have one Vote.

Immediately after they shall be assembled in Consequence of the first Election, they shall be divided as equally a
of the Senators of the first Class shall be vacated at the Expiration of the second Year, of the second Class at the Expiration
Class at the Expiration of the sixth Year, so that one third may be chosen every second Year; and if Vacancies happen by R
Recess of the Legislature of any State, the Executive thereof may make temporary Appointments until the next Meeting of th
such Vacancies.

No Person shall be a Senator who shall not have attained to the Age of thirty Years, and been nine Years a Citize
not, when elected, be an Inhabitant of that State for which he shall be chosen.

The Vice President of the United States shall be President of the Senate, but shall have no Vote, unless they be equally

The Senate shall chuse their other Officers, and also a President pro tempore, in the Absence of the Vice President, o
President of the United States.

The Senate shall have the sole Power to try all Impeachments. When sitting for that Purpose, they shall be on
of the United States is tried, the Chief Justice shall preside: And no Person shall be convicted without the Concurrence of two thir

Judgment in Cases of Impeachment shall not extend further than to removal from Office, and disqualification
Trust or Profit under the United States: but the Party convicted shall nevertheless be liable and subject to Indictment,
according to Law.

Section. 4. The Times, Places and Manner of holding Elections for Senators and Representatives, shall be presc
thereof; but the Congress may at any time by Law make or alter such Regulations, except as to the Places of chusing Sen

The Congress shall assemble at least once in every Year, and such Meeting shall be on the first Monday
appoint a different Day.

Section. 5. Each House shall be the Judge of the Elections, Returns and Qualifications of its own Members, and
Quorum to do Business; but a smaller Number may adjourn from day to day, and may be authorized to compel th
such Manner, and under such Penalties as each House may provide.

Each House may determine the Rules of its Proceedings, punish its Members for disorderly Behaviour, and,
Member.

Each House shall keep a Journal of its Proceedings, and from time to time publish the same, excepting such
Secrecy; and the Yeas and Nays of the Members of either House on any question shall, at the Desire of one fifth of those

Neither House, during the Session of Congress, shall, without the Consent of the other, adjourn for more tha
than that in which the two Houses shall be sitting.

Section. 6. The Senators and Representatives shall receive a Compensation for their Services, to be ascertaine
the United States. They shall in all Cases, except Treason, Felony and Breach of the Peace, be privileged from
Session of their respective Houses, and in going to and returning from the same; and for any Speech or Debate in e
any other Place.

No Senator or Representative shall, during the Time for which he was elected, be appointed to any civil
which shall have been created, or the Emoluments whereof shall have been encreased during such time; and no
States, shall be a Member of either House during his Continuance in Office.

Section. 7. All Bills for raising Revenue shall originate in the House of Representatives; but the Senate may pr

Every Bill which shall have passed the House of Representatives and the Senate shall, before it become a

Chapter One

We Have Independence. What Now?

In 1776, the nation's Founding Fathers signed the Declaration of Independence. The declaration boldly announced that the thirteen colonies would from now on be completely free from any political ties with Great Britain. This meant that these free and independent states had "full Power to levy War, conclude Peace, contract Alliances, establish Commerce, and to do all other Acts and Things which Independent States may of right do." It had not been easy to get the representatives of the thirteen colonies to agree to separate from Britain. However, that was nothing compared to getting this diverse and quarrelsome group to agree on what to do next.

Opposite: The Constitution of the United States of America helped make the united colonies the United States.

A First Stab at a Constitution

The Second Continental Congress, the body that agreed to the Declaration of Independence, was made up of representatives from the thirteen colonies. However, each of these colonies was as free and independent from each other as the colonies as a whole were now free from Great Britain. For the most part, they liked it this way. Each colony had its own government, its own currency, and even its own constitution. At this point in American history, the colonists didn't really think of themselves as Americans. They thought of themselves as citizens of their individual states. Thomas Jefferson once said, "Virginia, sir, is my country." When you think about it, this makes sense. At this point, there was no nation to feel a part of, just a loose affiliation of colonies.

As soon as the Declaration of Independence had been approved, the delegates to the Second Continental Congress

Prior to independence, the colonists had many opinions about British rule. Some opinions eventually helped form the United States.

got busy designing a government that would allow the colonies to work together as a political organization. They intended to keep the union rather loose, and did not want a strong central government. For many years, the monarchy and the parliament in London had trampled the rights of their colonies. This left the colonists very leery of handing a great deal of power to a government at home. Also, the fact that the colonies were scattered along the eastern seaboard made it difficult for them to truly feel like a single country. In those days before modern transportation and communication, Georgia was a very long way from Massachusetts. The economies, politics, and lifestyles of the colonies varied a great deal too. This made it difficult to create a system of government that suited everyone. The document they came up with was formally named the Articles of Confederation and Perpetual Union. Today it is most often called by its shorter name, the Articles of Confederation. It was the first constitution of the United States, but it did not last very long. The Articles of Confederation were adopted by the Second Continental Congress in 1777, but they were not ratified by all of the states until March 1, 1781—just two years before the end of the American Revolution. After ratification of the Articles, the Continental Congress was called the Confederation Congress.

Weak Words

The Articles didn't really do the job. Technically, they gave the central government a reasonable amount of power to take care of business. The Confederation Congress could manage the war, appoint military officers, make treaties with foreign nations, borrow money, and set the value of its own currency. In reality, however, the Congress had very little power—especially over the individual states. Congress could demand that the states send troops or pay money, but it had no way of enforcing these demands. The new government did not have an executive nor a judicial branch. According to the Articles, it took nine of the thirteen colonies to pass a law. This made it very difficult to pass any legislation. On top of that, Congress had only one chamber, and each state had one vote. Big states with large populations had no more votes than small states with few people. This system did not encourage the states to work together or compromise on issues that affected all of them. A few small states could prevent legislation that would affect far more people than just the citizens of their states. Meanwhile, the states showed little interest in cooperating with each other. Virginia, for example, passed a law that said it could confiscate the ships of other states if they did not pay taxes to Virginia!

Shipping and trade were particular points of conflict between the separate colonies.

It was obvious that the Articles of Confederation were far from ideal, but that didn't make much difference. The government had been intentionally designed to make it extremely unlikely that the colonies would make changes to the Articles. Not just nine, but all thirteen states had to agree if they wanted to make an amendment to the Articles. Getting unanimous agreement from this diverse and cantankerous collection of states was virtually impossible. Representatives couldn't be depended on to show up for votes. When they did, they argued with each other more than they worked. Though the Articles were almost useless, it seemed as if they were stuck with them.

And Furthermore

At the time of the Constitutional Convention, all thirteen colonies had their own armies, and nine of them had navies.

The situation was made much worse because of the war. The budding nation was at war with the largest empire in the world. This required a great deal of planning, organization, and money. The Articles did not provide any way for the central government to collect taxes from the states to pay for the war or anything else. Congress had no power to tax the citizens. They could ask for money from the states, but they couldn't make the states pay. More often than not, the states simply ignored these requests. This meant that the government often did not have money to pay the Revolutionary Army. They couldn't afford to pay for necessary food and supplies for the soldiers, so the army was chronically undersupplied. The currency printed by the central government was often worthless because there was no money to back it up. This story illustrates the problem:

This painting shows members of the Continental Army. Back then, army soldiers may have had trouble collecting their wages.

When the British surrendered to the Americans at Yorktown, Virginia, in 1781, a messenger was sent to Congress with news of the victory. Congress, obviously, welcomed the news. The government, however, had no money to pay the messenger. They passed the hat and collected enough money from the individual delegates to pay the messenger for his services.

After the war was over, things got worse. The 1783 Treaty of Paris that ended the war required Americans to pay any debts they owed to British citizens or businesses. Many British citizens who lived in the colonies but had remained loyal to Britain during the war had had their property confiscated.

According to the peace treaty, if debts owed to these loyalists weren't paid, the loyalists could go to court to have their property returned. This provision of the treaty was unpopular with the colonists who had supported the revolution. Many states simply refused to enforce it. In response, the British refused to leave military installations in the US territories. The ink on the peace treaty was barely dry, and the British and the colonies were already arguing again.

Because Congress did not have the power to regulate trade, British companies flooded the American market with British goods, making it difficult for American importers and manufacturers to make a profit. The states tried to impose import taxes on these goods, but that only made things more complicated, especially since the states all had different currencies and trade policies with each other and with Europe. Things were in an incredible mess. The loose confederation of states was completely dysfunctional. It was hard to see how things could get worse. Yet they were about to.

Mutiny

It's a very dangerous thing for a nation to be unable to pay its soldiers. In June 1783, four hundred revolutionary war soldiers arrived in Philadelphia and demanded their back pay. The war had ended in April of that year, and the soldiers wanted to be paid, and to be paid right then. The Philadelphia state house was then the home of Congress. (It is now known as Independence Hall.) According to the Articles of Confederation, the central government had no authority over the military other than in wartime. The central government could not order the soldiers to go home. They couldn't do anything about the Philadelphia

Independence Hall in Philadelphia holds a special place in colonial and revolutionary history.

mutiny, as it is sometimes called. State militias were in charge of keeping the peace, and Pennsylvania was unwilling to step in and disperse the mob of soldiers.

The soldiers meant business. They barricaded the delegates inside the meeting hall and refused to let them leave until they paid the soldiers what was owed them. Of course, Congress didn't have the money to pay! Alexander Hamilton, a delegate from New York, talked with the soldiers and convinced them to let the delegates out so that they could try to devise a solution. Meanwhile, Hamilton and a few other delegates sent a letter to the Pennsylvania government asking them to use their militia to protect the delegates when Congress was in session. If they refused (and they did), the government would have to find another place to meet.

The soldiers finally did free the delegates. Once they were released, they held secret meetings in several other locations—

And Furthermore

Alexander Hamilton was General Washington's personal aide during the American Revolution. He was killed in 1804 in a duel with US vice president Aaron Burr.

Maryland, New Jersey, and New York. They asked the states for money to pay the soldiers and other war debts. The states came up with a paltry amount that did nothing to help the situation.

The Congress asked George Washington, general of the Continental Army, for help. He recalled two generals, and sent troops to end the mutiny. However, it was only a temporary solution. Washington realized that the central government was far too weak, and the consequences of such a weak government could be disastrous. Washington said, "I ... predict the worst consequences from a half starved, limping Government, that appears to be always moving upon crutches & tottering at every step."

This illustration imagines the moments before Alexander Hamilton and Aaron Burr dueled.

More Rebellion

If the federal government couldn't tax the citizens, the state governments most certainly could—and they did. Businesses in Europe and America that had loaned the colonies money during the war were now demanding repayment. Because so much money was being spent to repay debts, there was little cash available in the states. Farmers were expected to pay high interest and meet very short repayment schedules on the loans they took out to plant their crops. This put many of them at risk of losing their farms. Taxes were also extremely high in many states. Many famers lost their land and some were thrown into debtors' prisons. A large number of these farmers were former soldiers in the Continental Army who hadn't been paid. Others were former members of state militias. The situation came to a head in Massachusetts in the summer of 1786. Daniel Shays, a former captain in the Continental

Government troops fire on rebels during Shays's Rebellion.

Army, led a group of former soldiers in a violent uprising in Massachusetts. The band of rebels mounted protests and blockades at courthouses so that debt collectors could not do their work. Other similar protests happened throughout the country, from New Hampshire to South Carolina. Washington's prediction was rapidly coming true. The young nation was falling apart before it had even begun.

In December, the governor of Massachusetts ordered the Massachusetts militia to quell the uprising. In January, Shays's group of twelve hundred men stormed the federal armory in Springfield, Massachusetts. When they arrived, they found fifteen hundred soldiers waiting for them. The soldiers fired on the rebels, who quickly retreated. Only a few were killed, and not many more injured. Even though Shays's Rebellion, as the event came to be known, was not successful, it clearly proved that the Articles of Confederation were not enough to keep the young nation together.

Cooler Heads

A group of the new nation's leaders called another convention, this time to try to repair the Articles of Confederation. They were not trying to put together a completely new and better constitution this time around. They were mainly aiming to address some of the issues with the Articles that made trade between the states difficult. The delegates who attended this meeting were primarily interested in the economics of interstate commerce. Twelve delegates from five states—Pennsylvania, New Jersey, New York, Delaware, and Virginia—met at Mann's Tavern in Annapolis, Maryland, in September 1786. Travel in those days was difficult. Delegates from New Hampshire,

Massachusetts, Rhode Island, and North Carolina were unable to make it to the meeting on time. Connecticut, Maryland, South Carolina, and Georgia didn't try to send delegates. The official name of the gathering was the Meeting of Commissioners to Remedy Defects of the Federal Government. The problem was there were a great many defects to remedy. Trade wasn't the half of it. Most leaders realized that something had to be done, even if it wasn't quite clear what that should be. Very little was accomplished in Mann's Tavern that week. However, the meeting was not a waste of time. The delegates made one very important decision. They decided to call for another meeting—a constitutional convention with aims far broader than dealing with interstate trade issues.

Though the Articles had deliberately created a weak central government, not all of the Founding Fathers were in favor of such a system. As the defects of the Articles became more apparent, these voices began to speak up. James Madison, George Washington, Alexander Hamilton, John Jay, and James Wilson had been working since the Articles were first adopted to strengthen the federal government. Letters between Madison and Washington show that the two men were carefully watching and waiting until the situation became desperate enough to justify their case for a strong federalist system. Shays's Rebellion (and similar uprisings in other states) provided just that opportunity. In addition, the economic problems of the new nation were reaching a crisis.

Now these Federalists, as they would come to be called, had a chance to create a new constitution that would provide the strong central government they believed was necessary. Alexander Hamilton sent a letter to each state legislature inviting them to send representatives to a convention in Philadelphia in May 1787. There they would address the problems of the Articles. The idea was met with general approval, but there was one big problem. George Washington did not want to attend. He very much supported the idea of a new constitution (and believed that a much stronger central government was necessary). However, his mother and sister were ill, and he was needed at Mount Vernon, his farm. Also, because he was so popular, it was likely that he would be elected president of the convention. He had already made it clear that he did not want to serve in public office. To turn down this position if it were offered might look churlish. To accept might suggest ambitions he did not have.

Some people feared that without Washington, the convention was doomed to failure. On the other hand, if Washington did attend and the meeting failed, would that doom the new nation once and for all? In the end, James Madison and Edmund Randolph, another good friend of Washington,

Mount Vernon was the home of the beloved general and eventual president George Washington.

persuaded the beloved general to attend the convention. And as expected, he was elected president of the convention.

However, there were powerful leaders who still opposed a strong central government—and opposed it fiercely. John Hancock and Patrick Henry were chief among these "Anti-Federalists." They were concerned about taking too much power from the states and giving it to the federal government. They believed that the problems with the Articles could be remedied without creating a powerful central government. They also worried that a strong central government would be just another form of monarchy. To create such a government, they thought, would merely replace one monarchy with another—the new monarch simply being a government instead of an individual.

George Washington sat in this chair during the drafting of the US Constitution.

After all the struggle to convince the colonies to separate from Great Britain and a bloody seven-year war for independence, the Founding Fathers still faced a very difficult task in putting together a government that would please everyone and yet be strong enough to unite the states. The Federalists knew that they would have to move carefully if they wanted to accomplish their goals. The war had been won; the colonies were independent. However, they weren't truly the United States quite yet.

The Final Push: Madison's Influence

Shays's Rebellion and other similar incidents had clearly shown that the Articles of Confederation were not good enough. Yet even at the beginning of the Constitutional Convention, many, if not most, delegates were still unconvinced that they needed to write a completely new constitution. Many were particularly opposed to a constitution that enshrined a strong central government. So what changed their minds? What was the final push that led to the document we have today?

Because the negotiations were kept secret, it is hard for us to know exactly how the debate went. We do know, however, what votes were held and how each delegate voted on the various items that came up for vote.

From these records, we also know that James Madison was the only delegate to attend every session of the convention. He made extensive notes, and these were published four years after his death—he requested that they not be published until after the deaths of all of the delegates. It is clear from Madison's notes and letters he wrote to colleagues both before and after the convention that Madison carefully and deliberately laid the groundwork for the Constitution we have today. He talked with—and listened to—the other delegates, made compromises, and worked deals in order to achieve his goals. This is one of the reasons that today we think of James Madison as the father of the United States Constitution.

Chapter Two

An Owners' Manual for the Government

It had taken almost four years to get the Articles of Confederation ratified. Getting an agreement on a new constitution would be an even bigger job, though it wouldn't take as long. The framers of the document wanted to be sure of two things: First, the document they came up with had to please enough of the people to be ratified. Second, it had to be strong enough yet flexible enough to keep the nation unified for a very long time. They managed it, but not without a great deal of debate and ultimately many compromises.

Mud and Secrets

The weather in Philadelphia in the spring of 1787 was dreadful. There was record rainfall. In some places the city's unpaved

Opposite: Benjamin Franklin addresses the Constitutional Convention.

streets turned into seas of mud. For most of the delegates, just getting to Philadelphia was an adventure. Travel in those days was difficult and inconvenient. These men were not full-time politicians. They were farmers, lawyers, and businesspeople. Attending this meeting took time away from work, as well as from home and family. They were meant to assemble on May 13, 1787. However, it was another two weeks before enough delegates had arrived to get down to business. Eventually, fifty-five delegates from twelve of the thirteen colonies gathered to try to find a solution to the problems of the Articles of Confederation. Rhode Island was the only colony that did not send anyone to the meeting. It didn't want to be a part of any plan that would increase the power of the central government.

These fifty-five men became known as the framers of the Constitution because they "framed," or built, the structure for what would become the Constitution of the United States.

Many delegates traveled to the Constitutional Convention in a horse-drawn carriage like this one.

Alexander Hamilton, James Madison, George Washington, George Mason, Elbridge Gerry, John Dickinson, and Benjamin Franklin were a few of the delegates we remember most today. Their deliberations were kept secret. The delegates closed themselves behind barred doors and locked windows to do their work. (And this was in an un-air-conditioned building in late spring and early summer in Philadelphia!) The delegates wanted to be able to freely express their opinions, change their minds, and make deals with each other. This would have been much harder to do if the proceedings had been public. They also feared that if the public saw the document in bits and pieces, they would give up on it before a final version was available.

And Furthermore

At the time of the Constitutional Convention, Philadelphia was the largest city in North America. It had a population of forty thousand people.

Some of the nation's most prominent founders were not at this meeting. Thomas Jefferson was serving as the nation's ambassador to France. John Adams was also out of the country, serving as ambassador to Great Britain. John Hancock, Samuel Adams, and Patrick Henry were also absent. Patrick Henry avoided the meeting for much the same reason Rhode Island did. Henry was a fierce Anti-Federalist. He was also alarmed that the meeting's proceedings were to be kept secret. "I smell a rat in Philadelphia," he said.

At the onset of the meeting, some of the delegates still hoped that the Articles could be rewritten and repaired. Others came to Philadelphia already convinced that the Articles would have to be scrapped and replaced with something that gave

Patrick Henry was an excellent orator and prominent Anti-Federalist. He was also suspicious of the Constitutional Convention.

far more power to the central government. These Federalists knew, however, that they needed to make their case carefully and slowly. There was a great deal of anti-federalist sentiment among the delegates, and many of them aimed, initially, to simply tweak and tinker with the Articles to shore up an essentially weak government.

James Madison, however, had other plans. He was convinced that the nation needed a strong central government, and he came to the convention determined to make that happen. Madison was not a typical charismatic leader. He was short of stature, had a weak voice, and was not in robust health. What he lacked in stage presence, however, he made up for in intellectual power. He had spent most of his life studying the forms of government of other nations, both historic and contemporary. Like many of the other Founding Fathers (particularly John Adams and Thomas Jefferson), he had read widely in political philosophy. He was familiar with the works of Enlightenment philosophers, such as John Locke and Montesquieu. Madison had also carefully studied the constitutions of the individual states. He knew what worked and what didn't, and what issues were important to each of the states. He knew which of the delegates were on

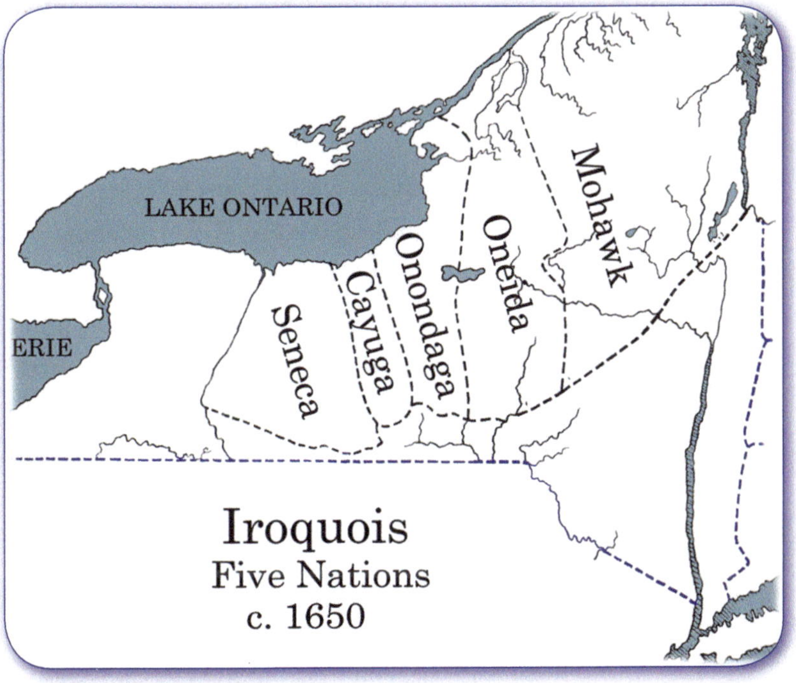

A map of the five nations that made up the Iroquois Federation. This group had an agreement in place that inspired the US Constitution.

And Furthermore

One of the influences on the framers of the US Constitution was the constitution of the Five Nations of the Iroquois Confederacy.

his side and which were not. Perhaps more importantly, he knew precisely what objections those who opposed him would make. He was prepared to make arguments that would convince them. He bided his time, and when the moment was right, he proposed a plan.

The Virginia Plan

Madison and fellow Virginia delegate Edmund Randolph proposed a plan called the Virginia Plan. Madison had done most of the work drafting the plan. It outlined a government with three branches: a legislative, an executive, and a judicial. The legislative branch would be bicameral, that is, divided into two chambers, or houses. In both of the legislative chambers, the number of representatives would be determined by population. Smaller states would have fewer representatives than larger states.

In the Virginia Plan, the central government was much stronger than in the Articles of Confederation. The central government would be in charge of settling disputes among states. Congress would also be responsible for electing the president and federal judges. The president would be able to veto (or refuse to sign) laws passed by the legislature. With enough votes in both houses, however, the legislature could reverse or override the veto. Many aspects of the Virginia Plan made it into the final Constitution. However, just as Madison had expected, his plan was not an easy sell.

Many delegates were troubled by the strong central government in the Virginia Plan. However, the plan's method of allocating representatives caused even more problems. As you might expect, the larger states liked the idea of giving more representatives to states with larger populations. The smaller states did not like the idea at all. On the one hand, it makes sense to give states with large populations more representatives. When representatives are allocated based on population, the people are more fairly represented. Each person, no matter where he or she lives, has an equal voice in Congress. On the other hand, smaller states worried that their interests as a state wouldn't be protected in such a scheme. The various states had much different economies, and commerce had long been a tricky issue between the states.

Nonetheless, James Madison (and others) strongly believed that equal representation among the states would be harmful to the majority of the people of the nation. Most people would have less representation in the national government than a few people living in small states. In the long run, such a scheme could (and did) cause many problems.

How many representatives each state would get was such a contentious issue that the Delaware delegation threatened to walk out of the convention over it. The entire project seemed to be falling apart because no one could agree on how to deal with the question of representation.

Compromises

In order to break the deadlock, delegates from New Jersey offered an alternative plan—the New Jersey Plan. Like the Virginia Plan, the New Jersey plan had three branches of government. However, it called for a single-chambered legislature. Each state, no matter its population, would have one vote. The New Jersey Plan also gave far less power to the federal government, though the central government could impose taxes and regulate trade. The New Jersey Plan wasn't really much help. It provided an alternative for those who wanted equal representation and a relatively weak central government. However, it didn't offer anything to persuade those who supported the Virginia Plan to agree to it. It was beginning to look hopeless. Leaders such as Benjamin Franklin, George Washington, and Alexander Hamilton were despairing of finding a solution. A compromise was needed, yet no one seemed willing to bargain. If the delegates had opened the doors and windows on this debate, the citizens might have given up all hope for a unified nation.

In early July, Congress appointed a committee to step aside from the larger group and see if they could come up with something that would work. Benjamin Franklin was chosen to be the chair. After great effort, the committee emerged with a new plan. It was called the Great Compromise. It was, for the most part, more like the Virginia Plan than the New Jersey Plan but had elements that would satisfy the smaller states that had favored the New Jersey Plan. According to it, Congress would have two houses. The upper house—called the Senate—would be made up of two representatives of each state, no matter the population. The lower house—the House of Representatives—would have a certain amount of representatives based on the population of each state.

The next problem the delegates had to address was how to go about determining the population of the states. This was trickier than it might have at first seemed. The Northern states were primarily manufacturing states. The Southern states were primarily agricultural. Their economies depended on slavery. The Southern slaveholding states were less populous than many of the Northern industrial states, but many of the people who lived there were slaves. If you counted slaves as part of the population, the Southern states would have far more representatives than if you didn't count them. The Southern states wanted to count slaves when determining how many representatives they would have in Congress. They did not want to count slaves when determining how much taxes they would pay to the central government. After all the committee's work, the whole thing looked like it was going to fall apart again over representation. But at last, a compromise was reached. James Wilson of Pennsylvania suggested what has become known as the Three-Fifths Compromise. It was determined that for

Carolina rice fields like this one required slave labor to be profitable.

purposes of both representation and taxation, slaves would count as three-fifths of a person.

Many of the Northern delegates were opposed to slavery. However, the Southern states' economic dependence on the despicable institution made it a useful tool for the other states when negotiating the details of the Constitution. For example, Southern states wanted bills about trade to require more than a simple majority of votes to pass. In order to get them to drop this demand, the Northern states agreed to a provision in which free states were required to return runaway slaves to slave states, and one that required the federal government to help suppress slave revolts. They also agreed to a provision that prohibited Congress from banning the international slave trade for another twenty years. These compromises were necessary to get enough states to agree to the Constitution to get it passed. However, not only were these provisions morally reprehensible, but they created problems for the future. Continuing the slave trade did nothing to help the Southern states develop economies that weren't dependent on slavery. Instead, it reinforced the institution of slavery. The runaway slave provision made it difficult for abolitionists in the North and the South to help relocate escaped slaves. Moreover, the Three-Fifths Compromise gave a great deal of political power to the slave states—much more than they would have had counting only the free people who lived there. Gouverneur Morris, a delegate representing Pennsylvania, said this about the Three-Fifths Compromise:

> *The inhabitant of Georgia and South Carolina who goes to the coast of Africa, and in defiance of the most scared laws of humanity tears away his*

fellow creatures from their dearest connections and damns them to the most cruel bondages, shall have more votes in a government instituted for protection of the rights of mankind, than the citizen of Pennsylvania or New Jersey who views with a laudable horror so nefarious a practice.

Gouverneur Morris was one of the few delegates to the Constitutional Convention who spoke forcefully about the evils of slavery.

On January 3, 2017, the 115th US Congress took the oath to uphold the Constitution, the ultimate law of the land.

Indeed, it did give slaveholding states a far greater voice. The outsized power of the Southern states would eventually lead to a bloody civil war seventy-five years later. At the time, however, the Founding Fathers could come up with no better way to build the nation. Without those compromises, perhaps, there would have been no union to fight for.

The Constitution Rules

In addition to working out the details of representation, the framers had to address the thorny problem of how much power the federal government would have. At this time, the states still thought of themselves as thirteen sovereign nations. Under the Articles of Confederation, the states had enjoyed a great deal of power. They could make treaties with other nations, print money, and fight wars—even against each other! The leaders of the states did not want to hand over this power to another government. They realized, though, that it was necessary. How much power and precisely what powers would be given to the central government and what powers would remain with the states was an even bigger issue than how representation would be allotted. The United States still struggles with this issue even today.

The Federalists, of course, wanted a strong central government, but just what this entailed had to be haggled over and debated just as the matters of representation had been. In the end, the Federalists won more points than the Anti-Federalists. According to the Constitution they eventually created, the federal government could declare war, issue currency, and regulate trade among the states. It could make treaties and negotiate the terms of peace with other countries. The states could not do these things on their own. However,

This drawing shows the United States Supreme Court hearing oral arguments in 2013.

the states were allowed to take care of matters that pertained just to their state. A state could regulate trade within the state; they could organize state and local governments however they liked; they were in charge of conducting elections; and they could establish schools and provide for the safety of their citizens.

Some responsibilities were shared. Both the federal government and the state governments had the right to levy taxes, set up courts, and build roads. However, when a state and the federal government had a disagreement about who should be in charge of what or how a legal matter would be decided, the Constitution itself would be the final arbiter. The supremacy clause (Article VI, clause 2) of the Constitution was meant to take care of any power struggles that might occur between the federal government and the states. It says that the Constitution and federal laws are the supreme law of the land. In any case of conflict between a state and the federal government, the federal government wins. However, this is only the case when those federal laws are in accord with the Constitution. Often over the years, the Supreme Court has had to step in and determine when a law is in keeping with the Constitution.

Balancing Act

Even those who wanted a powerful central government were concerned about the government getting too much power. They cleverly limited federal power by giving different responsibilities to the different branches of government. This is called separation of powers. The legislative branch is in charge of making laws. The executive branch is in charge of executing and enforcing those laws. The judicial branch is in charge of interpreting laws. However, each branch has the ability to restrain the others in some ways. This is called a system of checks and balances. It creates a delicate balance of powers among the three branches of government. If any branch begins to behave like a monarch, the other branches can step in and stop it. Here are a few examples of how that works.

The legislative branch, made up of the House of Representatives and the Senate, makes the laws. A law cannot go into effect, however, until the president, a member of the executive branch, signs it. If the president vetoes a piece of legislation, it will not become law. To keep veto power from giving the president too much control over legislation, the Constitution says that the legislature can override a presidential veto if it has enough votes. A two-thirds majority in both houses

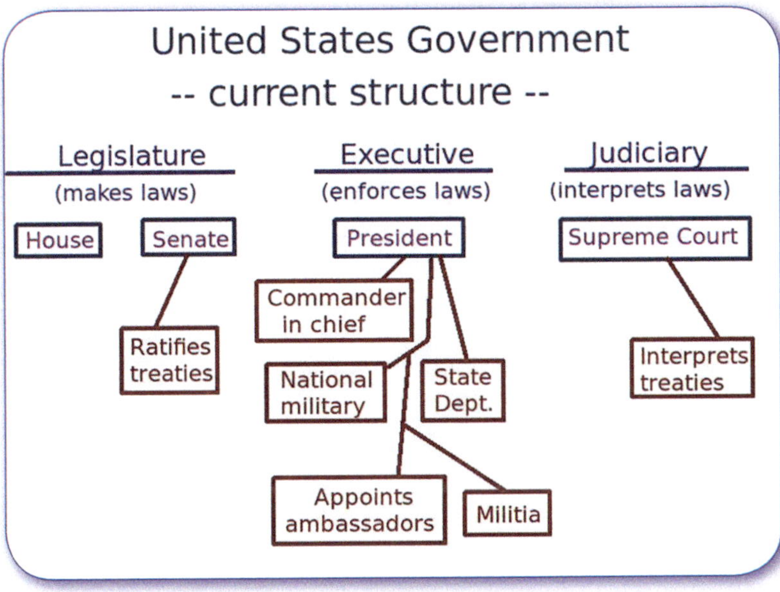

Here is an example of the balance of powers with respect to foreign policy.

of Congress is required to override a veto. (It doesn't happen often. On the other hand, presidents don't use their veto power all that often either.)

The executive branch is in charge of the military. The president is the commander-in-chief of all the armed forces. However, Congress—not the president—is in charge of declaring war and funding the military and wars. Congress also must approve all military appointments the president makes.

The judicial branch cannot make laws, but it can overturn them. The courts—particularly the Supreme Court—are responsible for making sure the laws that are passed are consistent with the Constitution. The Supreme Court can strike down any laws it determines are unconstitutional. However, Supreme Court justices are appointed by the president (executive branch) and those appointments are confirmed by the Senate (legislative branch).

The Constitution also allows for impeachment. When certain government officials, including the president, are determined to have committed a crime, abused their power, or violated the Constitution or their oath of office, Congress can bring them to trial before the Senate. If the Senate agrees that the accused is guilty of the charges, he or she is then removed from office.

This system of checks and balances is a powerful technique for preventing tyranny.

One Last Hurdle

The framers of the Constitution had worked out a plan for allocating representation, dividing the parts of government, and limiting the power of each branch. Now they had to convince the people back home to approve the document. The Constitution was written; now it had to be ratified by the states.

Despite all the compromises and intricate details, the document itself is fairly straightforward. The United States Constitution is divided into seven parts, called articles. Each article addresses one aspect of the government. Article I outlines the powers of the legislature; Article II, the powers of the executive branch; Article III, the powers of the judicial branch. Article IV explains the role of the states. Article V describes how to amend the Constitution. Article VI establishes that the Constitution is the supreme law of the land, and that federal law is supreme over state law. Article VII explains the process for ratifying the Constitution.

The Constitution contains just over forty-five thousand words (including signatures, but not amendments). The original document was only four pages long. If you are so inclined, you can keep a copy of it in the back pocket of your jeans. It is essentially a users' manual for the United States government. The framers of the Constitution were understandably proud of their work. However, the battle was not over. It would not become the supreme law of the land until at least nine of the thirteen states gave it their stamp of approval.

That turned out to be another major hurdle. It took one hundred days for the members of the Constitutional Convention to come up with a document that all the delegates could agree on. It took another three years to get all of the states to ratify the Constitution.

The Federalists had more or less carried the day at the convention. The new constitution did indeed create a strong central government. A majority of the delegates were convinced of federalism—enough to approve the Constitution. But many of the people in the states were still unconvinced. Anti-Federalists were opposed to the document because they thought it gave the central government far too much power. They wanted more protections for the rights and freedoms of individuals. The solution to this problem was to include a bill of rights. These spelled out certain freedoms and protections

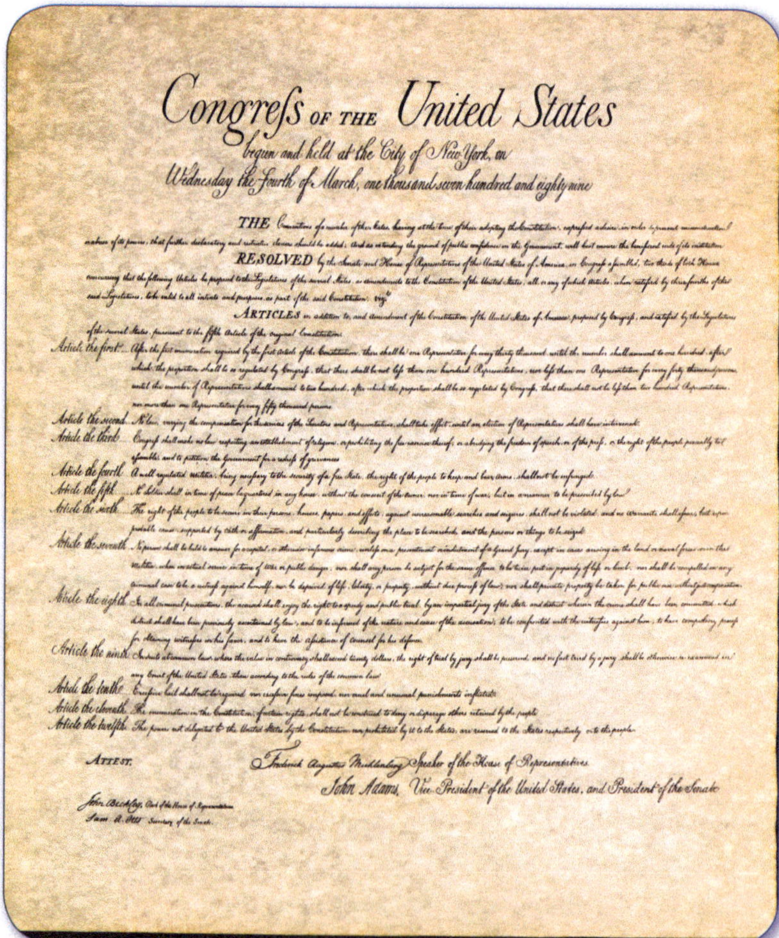

Congress of the United States
begun and held at the City of New-York, on
Wednesday the Fourth of March, one thousand seven hundred and eighty nine

THE
RESOLVED
ARTICLES

Attest,
John Adams, Vice-President of the United States, and President of the Senate

The United States Bill of Rights

Publius Has His Say

It wasn't easy to get the delegates at the Constitutional Convention to agree to a constitution that created such a federalist government. Getting the citizens of the states to ratify such a constitution proved even harder. The debate was especially fierce in New York.

Alexander Hamilton, a delegate from New York, was one of the strongest supporters of federalism. He decided to write a series of essays that would convince his fellow New Yorkers to support the Constitution. He wrote these essays under the pseudonym Publius and published them in New York newspapers. His fellow Federalists James Madison and John Jay soon joined the project. They also wrote under the name Publius. Between October 1787 and August 1788, these three men wrote eighty-five essays making the case for federalism. Hamilton wrote more than half of them. The essays were widely read both in New York and in other states. They were also published in a single volume called *The Federalist: A Collection of Essays Written in Favor of the New Constitution.*

These beautifully written essays convinced many doubters to support ratification. However, these writings have more than historical value. Today we call them the Federalist Papers, and they are often consulted when lawmakers and judges try to determine how best to interpret the Constitution.

that were guaranteed to the citizens. Many state constitutions already included them. George Mason had written the Virginia Declaration of Rights, and he argued that including a similar document as a part of the US Constitution would make it much easier to get ratification.

The Federalists did not want a bill of rights. They argued that any powers not specifically given to the federal government were held by the people (and the states). A bill of rights was unnecessary, they said. They also pointed out that listing specific rights might give the impression that those were the only rights that individuals had. Nonetheless, the demand for a bill of rights grew rapidly. Thomas Jefferson, in letters to James Madison, argued that because so many states included such protections, the people expected a bill of rights and would not be satisfied without one. The Constitution made no mention of the right to free speech and assembly, the right to worship as you pleased, or the right to a fair trial. People who opposed the Constitution wanted these and other rights specifically listed. Many states that did approve the Constitution added a request for a bill of rights to their ratification statements.

James Madison, a federalist, didn't agree with Jefferson at first. He responded to Jefferson saying that he liked the idea of spelling out specific rights, but he saw no need of it in the new Constitution. In the end, however, he wrote the Bill of Rights himself. Since the Constitution had already been approved and even ratified by some states, it was too late to change the wording of the document. In 1789, Madison provided a set of seventeen amendments to the Constitution. The Senate approved twelve of the amendments in 1789. By

December 1791, ten of these had been ratified by the states. These first ten amendments became the United States Bill of Rights. It had been a long struggle, with many setbacks and compromises, but the new nation finally had a constitution that united them.

Years later, James McHenry, a delegate to the Constitutional Convention, recalled that once the new constitution had been drafted, Benjamin Franklin stepped outside the hall to a waiting crowd. A woman called out to the great statesman, "Well, what have we got, a monarchy or a republic?" Franklin replied, "A republic, if you can keep it." The people of the United States have been working ever since to keep the republic enshrined in our constitution.

Chapter Three

The Constitution: A Work in Progress

It's hard to overstate how truly remarkable the United States Constitution is. It is the both the oldest and the shortest written constitution in the world. Many other nations have used the US Constitution as a model for their own. It has held together a diverse and often squabbling nation for more than two hundred years. Yet it is not a perfect document. We the people of the United States have been tweaking and interpreting our constitution ever since the ink was dry on the parchment.

Which People, Exactly?

The preamble—the introductory paragraph—of the Constitution are the first words of the original document, but they were the last to be written:

Opposite: A man and his young son look carefully at a copy of the US Constitution in the National Archives.

> *We the People of the United States, in Order to form a more perfect Union, establish Justice, insure domestic Tranquility, provide for the common defense, promote the general Welfare, and secure the Blessings of Liberty to ourselves and our Posterity, do ordain and establish this Constitution for the United States of America.*

Gouverneur Morris, a delegate from Pennsylvania, wrote the preamble himself. He wanted it to clearly explain the purpose of the Constitution. He also wanted it to give to the very diverse and widely scattered population of the new country a sense of belonging to one nation, of being united.

This was the first time the various states had been referred to as the United States. It is remarkable that delegates who entered the Pennsylvania State House as representatives of thirteen states—states that thought of themselves as independent nations—emerged as representatives of a unified country.

The phrase "We the People" is less astonishing but equally significant. Eleven years earlier, the Declaration of Independence had made clear that the people of this young country meant to govern themselves. "We the People" put that notion at the head of the document that is now the supreme law of the land.

The phrase "We the People" is a powerful statement about the philosophy and intent of the Constitution. However, the new government did not, in fact, represent all of the people. While the union was certainly "more perfect" than it had been under the Articles of Confederation, it fell far short of perfection. At that time, many of the people in the nation were slaves. They had no rights. Though a slave was counted as three-fifths of a person when it was convenient to his or her masters, he or she could not vote, could not serve in government, and could not have any say in running the country. The same was true of Native Americans, women, and even men who did not own property. In the early days of the nation, "We the People" was a small and exclusive group.

However, the Constitution did not specifically say who "We the People" were. It left that definition open for later generations. Forming a "more perfect union," was something that would take a lot of time and hard work. The Constitution was designed to allow for that. Article V provided a way to amend the Constitution. In the years to come, many changes would be made using the process of amendment.

The Thirteenth Amendment was ratified in 1865. It at last abolished slavery. In 1868, the Fourteenth Amendment gave equal protection under the law to all people. The equal

Americans of every gender, race, color, and background queue up to vote in 2016.

In 1912, two young women march for their right to vote.

protection clause of this amendment has been understood to protect the rights of many people fighting for their rights—African Americans, women, LGBT citizens, and any other citizen. The Fifteenth Amendment, ratified in 1870, prohibited states from denying voting rights to citizens because of their race or because they had previously been slaves. This was later understood to protect the voting rights of Native Americans as well. In 1920, the Nineteenth Amendment gave women the right to vote.

Even though the Constitution did not specifically define who "We the People" are, we the people have been defining that ever since.

Who Votes for the President?

Other changes have been made over the years. For example, initially state legislatures elected Senators. Now they are elected by popular vote. The Twelfth Amendment changed the way we elected presidents and vice presidents. Before 1804, electors voted for two presidential candidates. The one who received the most votes became president; the one who came in second was vice president. The Twelfth Amendment changed this so that we now vote separately for the two offices. The Twenty-Second Amendment, ratified in 1951, also made important changes to the presidency. Before that, as long as he or she continued to be elected, a president could serve an unlimited number of terms. The Twenty-Second Amendment limited that to two terms.

And Furthermore

George Washington and James Madison were the only two signers of the Constitution who would later become president.

One thing that has not been changed since 1787 is the electoral college. When a citizen casts a vote for president, he or she is not voting directly for the person he or she hopes will become president. Instead, each candidate is assigned

That Took a Long Time

Amending the Constitution is not easy. If we could change the Constitution willy-nilly, every time the political winds shifted, the Constitution wouldn't be very strong. On the other hand, if we couldn't change it at all, it wouldn't be flexible enough to withstand real, long-term changes in society. Once an amendment is proposed, it has to be ratified by three-quarters of the states. How long they have to do this, however, varies. In 1982, Gregory Watson, then a nineteen-year-old college student in Texas, found out that in some cases, it can be a very long time. Watson was researching the Constitution for a class paper. He discovered an interesting amendment that had been proposed but never ratified. The amendment said that if Congress voted to give itself a raise, that raise would not go into effect until after the next election. It was written in 1789 by James Madison himself! This amendment didn't have a deadline for ratification.

Watson decided that he would get it ratified. Thirty-eight states were needed to reach the three-quarter threshold. Nine states had already ratified it (most of them way back in the 1790s), so he needed only twenty-nine more.

Watson wrote dozens of letters to state lawmakers and eventually convinced enough of them to introduce the amendment in their state legislatures. In May 1992, the Michigan state legislature became the thirty-eighth state to ratify.*

* It was later discovered that a tenth state, Kentucky, had actually ratified the amendment in the 1790s, so officially Alabama (which also ratified in 1992) was the state that put the amendment over the top.

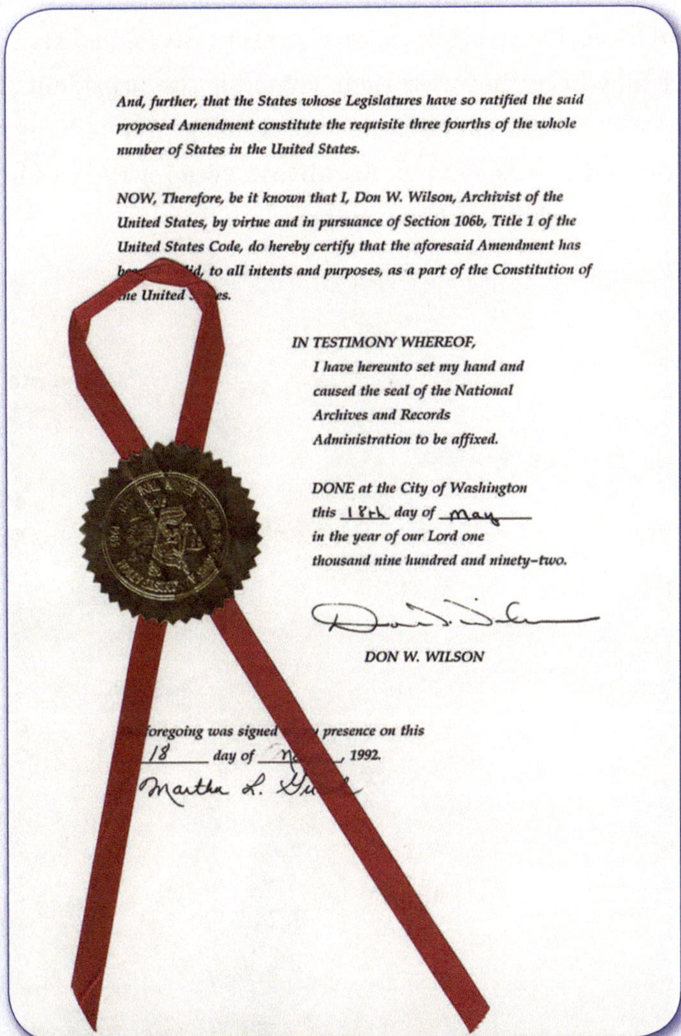

And, further, that the States whose Legislatures have so ratified the said proposed Amendment constitute the requisite three fourths of the whole number of States in the United States.

NOW, Therefore, be it known that I, Don W. Wilson, Archivist of the United States, by virtue and in pursuance of Section 106b, Title 1 of the United States Code, do hereby certify that the aforesaid Amendment has be[illegible]lid, to all intents and purposes, as a part of the Constitution of [illegible]e United [illegible]es.

IN TESTIMONY WHEREOF,
I have hereunto set my hand and caused the seal of the National Archives and Records Administration to be affixed.

DONE at the City of Washington this 18th day of May in the year of our Lord one thousand nine hundred and ninety-two.

DON W. WILSON

[illegible] foregoing was signed [illegible] presence on this 18 day of [illegible], 1992.

Martha L. [illegible]

This is the official certification of the Twenty-Seventh Amendment to the United States Constitution.

More than two hundred years after it was proposed, and ten years after Watson began campaigning for it, the Twenty-Seventh Amendment became law.

electors. Each state gets a number of electors based on its population. These electors, or representatives, are sent to a meeting where they cast their votes for the president. This body of electors is called the electoral college. Though they are not required to, they virtually always vote for the candidate the voters back home have chosen.

Al Gore won the popular vote but lost the electoral college vote in 2000.

It would take another amendment to the Constitution to eliminate the electoral college and allow direct election of presidents. Many people think this is a change that is way overdue—others aren't so sure.

The electoral college was designed to make presidential elections more direct, not less. The first plan had been for Congress to elect the president. However, some delegates feared this would give too much power to the legislative branch. Besides, it would be hard to get the people to support ratification if they were not involved in the election of the president. The electoral college was the solution. In the early days of the nation, when travel and communications weren't what they are now, it was a good solution. Voters in, say, South Carolina, might have trouble learning much about a candidate from Massachusetts. However, they could choose a local representative to vote for them. As the nation has grown and changed, though, the flaws of the system have become more apparent. In order to win the presidency, a candidate has to win the majority of electoral votes. Today that is 538 votes—270 for a win. A candidate can get to this number by winning a few big states (with lots of electoral votes) by a very narrow margin—and losing all the other states. This gives a disproportionate amount of electoral power to a few states. A candidate could be elected president if every single person in thirty-nine of the fifty states (and the District of Columbia) voted against him

And Furthermore

Jacob Shallus was an assistant clerk in the Pennsylvania Legislature in 1787. It was he who copied out, with quill on parchment, the first complete copy of the US Constitution.

This building is the home of the Supreme Court of the United States.

or her, as long as he or she won at least a slim majority of the other eleven states whose electoral votes add up to 270. (In all but two states, the winner of the election gets all the electoral votes—even if he or she wins by a small margin.) Five times in the history of the country the candidate who won the most votes of the people lost the election. This happened twice in the twenty-first century, in the elections of 2000 and 2016.

Not everyone agrees that the system needs to be changed, however. Almost everyone agrees that everyone should have an equal voice in electing the president. However, there are still regional differences in the country. Populations are higher in urban, coastal areas than they are in the rural central part of the country. Some people fear that electing a president by popular vote would result in giving more say to urban voters than rural ones. The argument is similar to the one that took place in those stifling rooms in Philadelphia in 1787. How do we arrange a government so that each person's voice carries as much weight as anyone else's? Like so many other issues, it is one that we will have to work out together.

The Constitution: Dead or Alive

There are many views about how the US Constitution should be interpreted. Some people say that we should interpret it based on the intent of the Founding Fathers. Others say that this is impractical. We can't ever know exactly what the framers intended, and clearly, they all had different views.

Some people say that the Constitution is a "living document" that changes—and should change—as our nation changes. Others say, not so fast! If the meaning of the Constitution keeps changing, what good is it?

Some people say that when determining what the Constitution means, we should go only by the words in the document itself. However, the meanings of words change as society changes, and the framers left a lot of things intentionally vague. For example, they didn't say what they meant by "people." Later generations have had to define that. The framers wanted the government of the United States to last a long time, and they deliberately designed a constitution that was flexible enough to work as well in the twenty-first century as it did in the eighteenth century. They trusted future generations to interpret the document in a responsible way.

When the Articles of Confederation proved too weak to unite the states, the people realized they needed a ruler, so they created one. It was not a monarch. It was not a person. It was a four-page document. It was created by the people and for the people, and could be adjusted as the people thought necessary. It could also be scrapped and replaced with a new one, if it proved as useless as the Articles of Confederation had. For two and a quarter centuries, it has united people into one remarkable union.

The US Constitution is not and never will be perfect. It is a work in progress, and perhaps the best thing about it is that "We the People" are the ones doing the work.

Glossary

abolitionist Someone who is in favor of and working toward ending the practice of slavery.

allocate To distribute, usually according to a specific method, people, items, or jobs.

amend To change or modify, usually a legal document.

Anti-Federalist A person who favored a weak central government with more power given to individual states.

arbiter One who decides an issue or settles a dispute.

bicameral Having two branches or chambers, usually referring to a legislative body; for example, the US House and Senate.

commerce Trade and trading relationships between people, states, or nations.

confederation An allied group of nations or organizations.

currency Something that is used as a medium of exchange; for example, the US dollar.

delegate A person who acts on behalf of others at a meeting or convention.

Enlightenment A philosophical movement that valued individual reason and autonomy over traditional authority.

federalism A system of government in which the power structure is shared between a strong central (federal) government and weaker local authorities.

Federalist A person who favored a strong central government.

impeachment Charging an office holder with impropriety or abuse of office.

judicial Having to do with justice, or the court system.

legislation Laws or a body of laws enacted by a governing body, such as the US Congress.

monarchy A form of government with a single, usually hereditary ruler, usually a king or queen, at its head.

preamble An introductory statement.

pseudonym A false name, often used by authors.

ratify To officially agree to or sign off on.

sovereign Independent, answering only to oneself.

veto To reject a law, proposal, or idea.

Further Information

Books

Elish, Dan. *James Madison*. Presidents and Their Times. New York: Cavendish Square, 2008.

Hennessey, Jonathan. *Alexander Hamilton: A Graphic History of an American Founding Father*. Berkeley, CA: Ten Speed Press, 2017.

Keegan, Anna. *The United States Constitution and Bill of Rights: The Law of the Land*. New York: Rosen Central, 2016.

Levinson, Cynthia, and Sanford Levinson. *Fault Lines in the Constitution: The Framers, Their Fights, and the Flaws That Affect Us Today*. Atlanta, GA: Peachtree, 2017.

Mooney, Carla. *The US Constitution: Discover How Democracy Works*. White River Junction, VT: Nomad, 2016.

SparkNotes. *(No Fear) US Constitution and Other Important Documents*. New York: SparkNotes, 2018.

Websites

The Avalon Project of Yale Law School

http://avalon.law.yale.edu/subject_menus/fed.asp

This link is to a collection of the Federalist Papers, but this site also has a wealth of founding documents, including many of James Madison's papers.

Congress for Kids

http://www.congressforkids.net/Constitution_index.htm

This site is aimed at middle grades and provides a lot of information and images about the history of the Constitution and current Congress.

Library of Congress

https://www.loc.gov/collections/continental-congress-and-constitutional-convention-from-1774-to-1789/articles-and-essays/timeline/1764-to-1765

This website contains a timeline and documents from the Continental Congress and the Constitutional Convention.

National Archives

https://www.archives.gov/founding-docs/declaration-transcript

Here you can find transcripts and high-resolution images of the Articles of Confederation, the Constitution, and other founding documents.

Bibliography

Amar, Akhil Reed. *America's Constitution: A Biography*. New York: Random House, 2005.

Applebaum, Yoni. "American's Fragile Constitution," *Atlantic*, December 12, 2017. https://www.theatlantic.com/magazine/archive/2015/10/our-fragile-constitution/403237.

Azerrad, David. "How James Madison Saved the Constitution by Writing the Bill of Rights," *The Federalist*, December 28, 2016. http://thefederalist.com/2016/12/28/james-madison-saved-constitution-month-writing-bill-rights.

Bilder, Mary Sarah. *Madison's Hand: Revising the Constitutional Convention*. Cambridge, MA: Harvard University Press, 2015.

Davidson, James West, et al. *Nation of Nations: A Narrative History of the American Republic*. Boston, MA: McGraw Hill, 2005.

Hamilton, Alexander, James Madison, and John Jay. *The Federalist Papers*. New York: Bantam, 1988.

Hogeland, William. *Founding Finance: How Debt, Speculation, Foreclosures, Protests, and Crackdowns Made Us a Nation*. Austin, TX: University of Texas Press, 2012.

Johnson, Paul. *A History of the American People.* New York: HarperCollins, 1997.

Ketchum, Ralph, ed. *The Anti-Federalist Papers and the Constitutional Convention Debates: The Clashes and the Compromises that Gave Birth to Our Form of Government.* New York: Signet Classic, 1986.

Klarman, Michael J. *The Framers' Coup: The Making of the United States Constitution.* Oxford, UK: Oxford University Press, 2016.

Marshall, Thurgood. Bicentennial Speech, Maui Hawaii, May 6, 1987. ThurgoodMarshall.com. http://thurgoodmarshall.com/the-bicentennial-speech.

Montgomery, Dennis. "Thomas Jefferson, Son of Virginia." *Colonial Williamsburg Journal*, volume 15, no. 3 (Spring 1993). http://www.history.org/foundation/journal/jeffart.cfm.

Posner, Richard. "Defending the Electoral College: Five Reasons to Keep Our Despised Method of Choosing the President." *Slate*, November 12, 2012. http://www.slate.com/articles/news_and_politics/view_from_chicago/2012/11/defending_the_electoral_college.html.

Robertson, David Brian. *The Original Compromise: What the Constitutions' Framers Were Really Thinking.* Oxford, UK: Oxford University Press, 2013.

Rosen, Jeffrey. "Interpreting the Constitution in the Digital Era," *Fresh Air*, National Public Radio, November 30, 2011. https://www.npr.org/2011/11/30/142714568/interpreting-the-constitution-in-the-digital-era.

Slonim, Shlomo. *Forging the American Nation, 1787–1791: James Madison and the Federalist Revolution*. New York: Palgrave McMillan, 2017.

White, Adam J. "'We the People' and Constitutional Liberty," *Weekly Standard*, July 11, 2016. http://www.weeklystandard.com/we-the-people-and-constitutional-liberty/article/2003234.

Wood, Gordon S. *The Idea of America: Reflections on the Birth of the United States*. New York: Penguin, 2011.

———. *The Radicalism of the American Revolution: How a Revolution Transformed a Monarchical Society into a Democratic One Unlike Any That Had Ever Existed*. New York: Knopf, 1992.

———. *Revolutionary Characters: What Made the Founders Different*. New York: Penguin, 2006.

Index

Page numbers in **boldface** are illustrations.

About the Author

Avery Elizabeth Hurt has written many books for children and young adults. If she had a time machine, she would almost certainly go back to the period just after the American Revolution when the nation's founders were working so hard to design the government we have now. Since she does not, she is planning a visit to Independence Hall in Philadelphia, Pennsylvania.